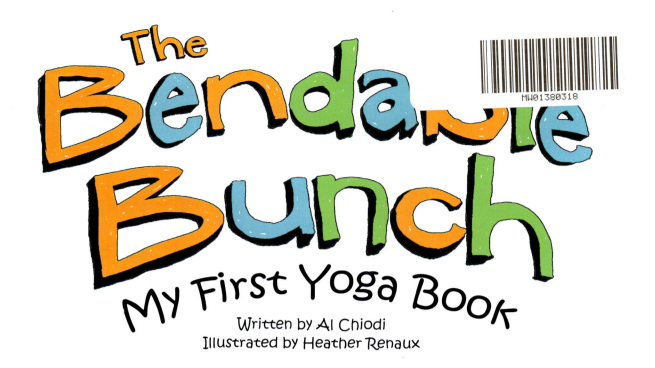

# The Bendable Bunch
## My First Yoga Book

Written by Al Chiodi
Illustrated by Heather Renaux

I pretend, with my friends,
that we're a bunch of creatures.
We bend, we flex, we twist around,
with Nature as our teacher.

Aren't we all a bendable bunch?
You can do your yoga with us.
Read along and have some fun.
All it takes is practice!

**Always do Yoga with a parent or teacher**

Coyote Press

# Boat

Floating here in my puddle,
I pretend that I am a boat.
It helps me stretch my back out
and the mud's good for my coat!

# Bow

On my tummy, I bend my knees,
my heels move toward my bottom.
I grasp my feet with my hands.
It's hard, but ... there, I got 'em!

# Bridge

I live right here in paradise,
high upon this mountain ridge.
In the mornings I bend and twist.
My favorite pose is "bridge."

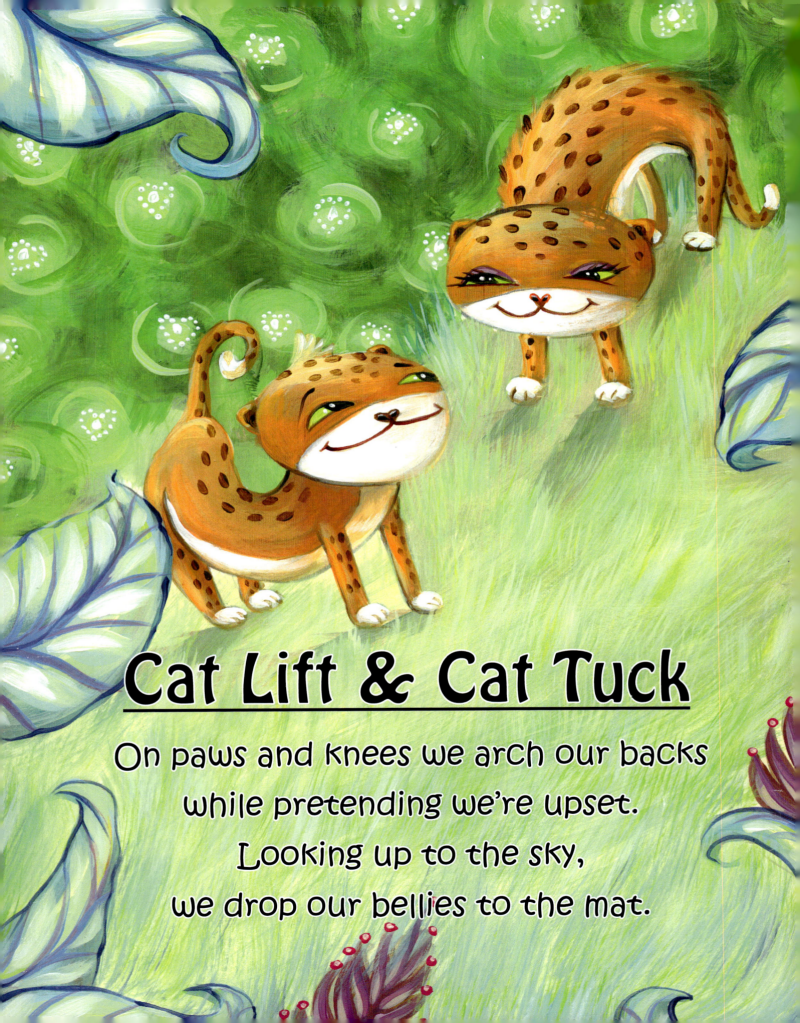

# Cat Lift & Cat Tuck

On paws and knees we arch our backs
while pretending we're upset.
Looking up to the sky,
we drop our bellies to the mat.

# Cow Face

I twist my arms and my legs
to look just like a cow's face.
I'm not sure I've done it right.
Please take a picture just in case.

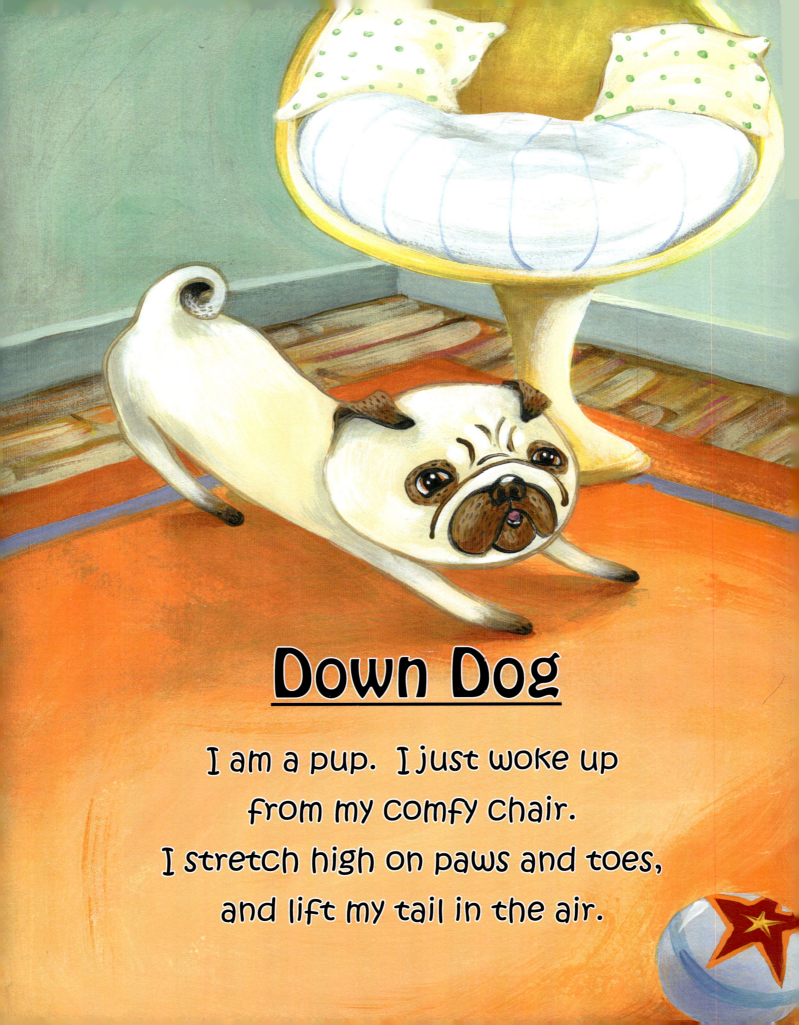

# Down Dog

I am a pup. I just woke up
from my comfy chair.
I stretch high on paws and toes,
and lift my tail in the air.

# Eagle

I am a little kitten.
Yet, a pretzel I am not.
This "eagle" pose gets me twisted
in a very funny knot!

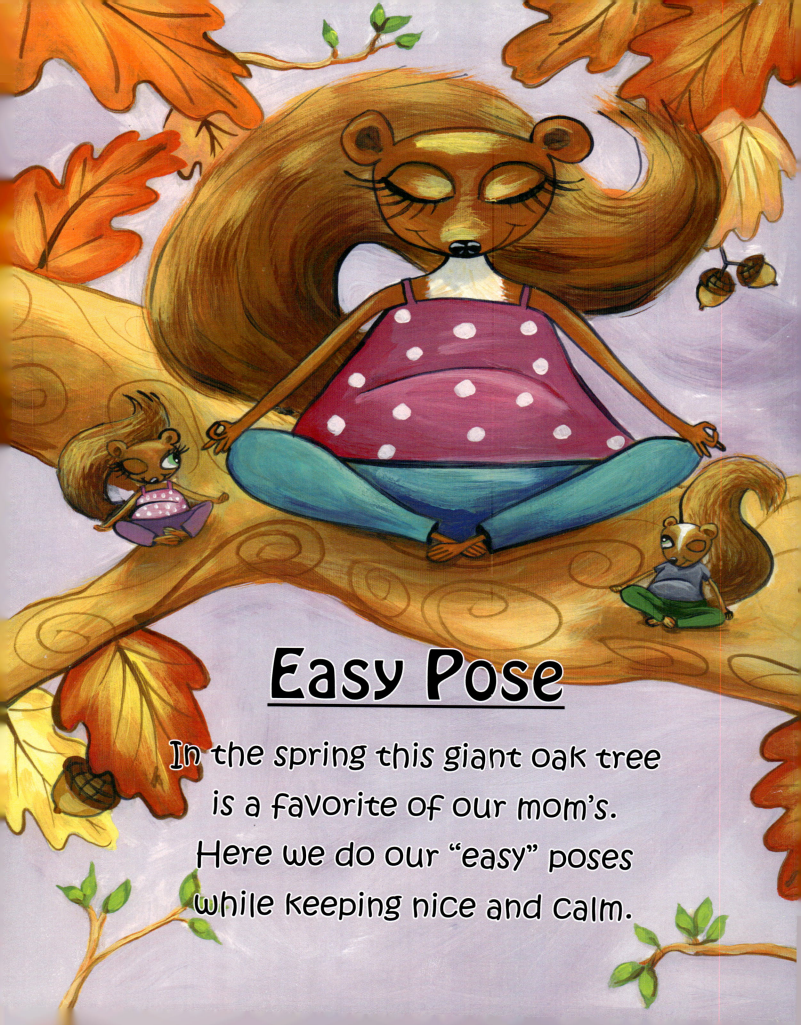

# Half Moon

One peaceful night in early June,
as crickets sing a Yoga tune,
I pretend I'm half a moon
and gaze upon the stars.

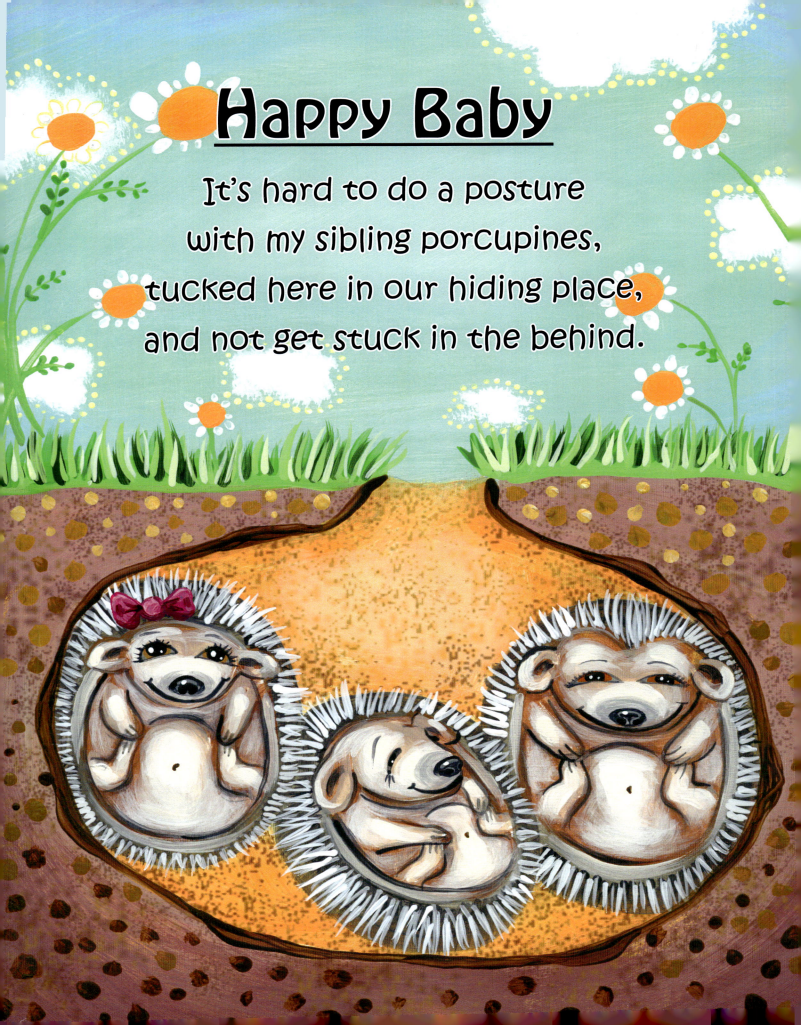

# Monkey

I am strong and very large;
practicing Yoga keeps me fit.
Sometimes I might lose my balance,
but that's just part of it.

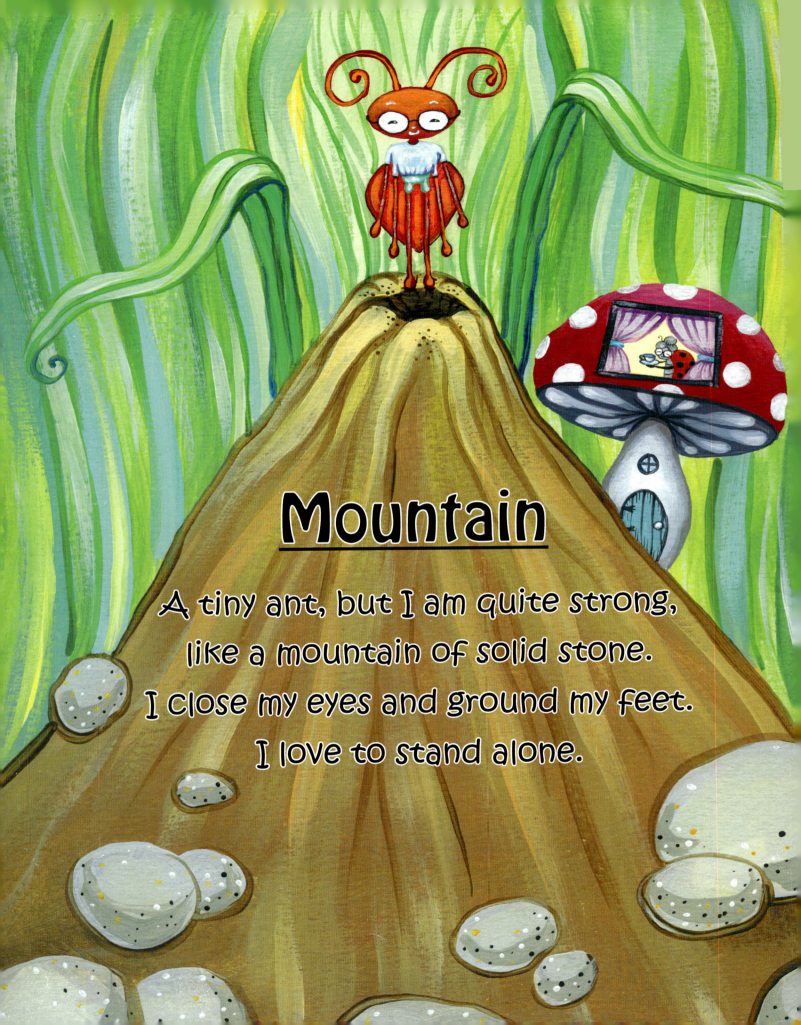

# Pigeon

Though city streets are busy,
my rug fits nicely on this space.
Some say one can do Yoga
any time or place.

# Prayer

My friends and I are grateful

we spend this time together.

Though we grow up and go our own ways,

we'll be friends forever.

# Savasana

There's no calmer place on Earth
than the center of this flower.
I relax but don't fall asleep.
I'll lie here for an hour.

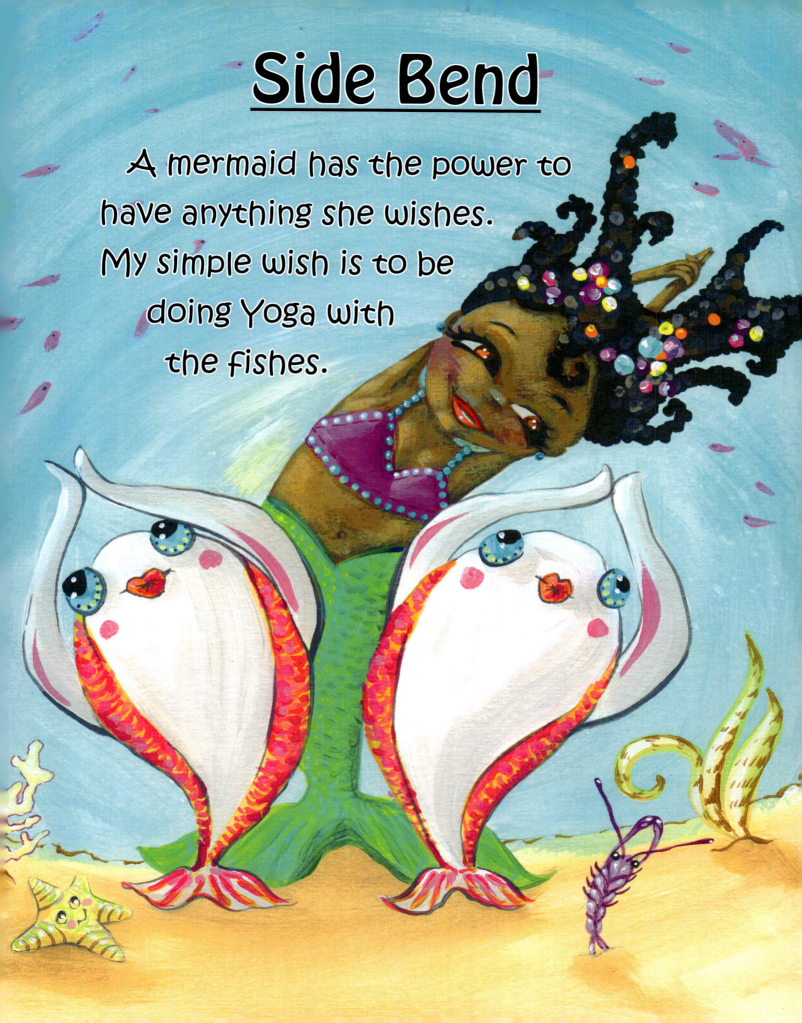

# Sphinx

A mighty sphinx that never blinks,
I gaze far across the plains.
I'll be here for a thousand years,
unless, of course, it rains!

# Tree

On lily pads, we act like trees
and we haven't fallen off yet.
Carefully we focus or
we wind up getting wet!

# Triangle

Here I am in "triangle."
It is my favorite pose.
And if I practice it just right,
I'll come out smelling like a rose.

# Warrior II

A strong and fluffy warrior,
I aim to keep my poise.
And to balance peace with power
and the silence with the noise.

*For Gale, Abi and ZiQin, who are fantastic poets.*
*-A.C.*

*This book is lovingly dedicated to the most wonderful husband and daughters in the world, Christian, Billie Rose, and Sophia.*
*-H.R.*

## The Author:

Al Chiodi loves making up mystery stories for his two girls, ZiQin & Abi. With his wife, Gale, they enjoy organic gardening, traveling to far off places, and hanging around the house with three spoiled cats. This is Al's fifth book and his first for children.

# Coyote Press
## USA

Coyote Press
PO Box 1758, Mount Dora, Florida 32756

Copyright © 2010 by Coyote Press
Text copyright © 2010 by Al Chiodi
Illustrations copyright © 2010 by Heather Renaux
Visit the illustrator at www.HeatherRenaux.com.
All rights reserved.
No part of this book may be reproduced or utilized in any form or by any means, electronic or manual, including photocopying, recording, or by information storage and retrieval system, without written permission from the publisher.

ISBN 978-0-9663285-7-8

10 9 8 7 6 5 4 3 2 1

Printed in the U.S.A.

## The Illustrator:

Heather Renaux is an artist who lives with her awesome husband, Chris, her two magical daughters, Billie & Sophia and their very loving cat, Lola.

You can visit Heather at:
www.HeatherRenaux.com

# www.TheBendableBunch.com